SIMPLE LATIN

Introduction

This Guide is intended for the family historian who has never learnt any Latin, or whose memory does not retain any of the standard words which are regularly found in parish registers. You may have looked at early registers and despaired of ever finding out which strange phrase hides the identity of your eighth great grandfather, but take courage. There was the occasional clergyman who was a well-educated Classics man and spattered his registers with Latin comments on the weather and the state of his soul, but most confined their Latin to the basic names, relationships and dates. A lot of clergy and practically all of the parish clerks who used Latin before the order went out not to do so, in 1733, managed with a remarkably small vocabulary AND SO CAN YOU.

Sometimes, they used words which were not proper Latin at all, but looked and sounded impressive. I have given examples of the form in which you will come upon words and phrases in common use, in parish registers, some of which you would never find in a normal dictionary, or even one of the various Late Latin historical word lists. I have also included a Latin will probate, with a short cut to extracting the meat without choking on the carbohydrate.

I have not included words from other Latin documents, for which you really need a grasp of the grammar and construction of the language, or any terms which occur in mediaeval source material, since I felt that by the time you are into hawking and hunting or the more obscure terms from legal disputes or manor court books, you will be far beyond the scope of this simple guide. There is a bibliography of Latin word lists recommended for further reading when you have reached this stage.

Latin Christian names

Some names look familiar to everyone. As a general rule, boys' names end in '-*us*', '-*is*' or '-*es*', girls' names in '-*a*' or '-*ia*' or '-*ix*', and by cutting off the endings, you can guess the modern form. Some are rather more obscure than this. Welsh and Scots names have often been Latinised without reference to their real meaning, using what looks like the nearest English form as the equivalent. These are included in the list with '(W)' or '(Sc)' against them.

The use of Latin in English documents was officially ended in 1733, though some clergy perversely carried on using it after that, especially for rude marginal comments on their flock. Catholic registers were kept in Latin long after this. Irish names had already been altered from Gaelic into an 'English' spelling and the Latinisation was based on the anglicised version. I have included some of these names, after '(Ir)' to indicate that the Latin should be translated this way in Irish Catholic records only.

There are several names of which the Latin form later became used as a name in its own right, so that the temptation is to read it as if the child was familiarly known by a name they had probably never even heard of. For instance, before 1700, all girls listed as 'Maria' were really 'Mary' to their families. Even Queen Henrietta Maria was called 'Queen Mary' in English (or 'Marie' in her native French).

However, a few upper class families adopted the Latin version of the name in the early or mid 1700's and this usage percolated downwards, without the knowledge that these names were just translations, so that after 1800, you may find sisters named Mary and Maria, or Eliza and Elizabeth. Several Latin based names became popular in the nineteenth century, mainly in the middle and upper classes, and I have indicated this by adding '(sep. name C19)'. The most popular names, Maria, Eliza, Anna, took root in the lower middle class late in the eighteenth century, as did Johanna to a lesser degree. Matilda, formerly the Latin version of the obsolete Maud, had a small vogue from the early years of the 1800's.

Before 1733 in Church of England registers, and generally in Catholic ones, all names in Latin should be translated into the current English, Irish, Scots or Welsh equivalent. Sometimes, one Latin version has to do duty for two differently derived English or Bible names — '*Anna*', for instance, can be Anne or Hannah. '*Jacobus*' is peculiarly awkward, since although it is generally used for James (hence 'Jacobites' for followers of James II's heirs) it also does duty for a genuine Jacob, which name came into limited vogue in Commonwealth times. The best rule is to think of it as James, but reserve judgement and see if the name Jacob occurs in that particular family after 1733.

Some Latin Christian Names

The English versions would be what the child was actually called at home at the time. Names which died out are marked 'obs.' for obsolete.

Abbreviations

Abbrev.	=	abbreviated form
obs.	=	obsolete name
rev.	=	revived use
m	=	male form
f	=	female form
C18	=	1700-1799

C19	=	1800-1899, *etc).*
sep.	=	*Latin form used as separate Christian name from date shown*
rare	=	*not often found, but awkward when it is*

Adamus - Adam
Adria - Audrey or short for *Adrianus*
Adrianus - Adrian
Aegidius - Giles (*Aegidia* for girls in Scotland)
Aemilius - (W) Emlyn
Aeneas - (Sc) Angus
Agneta - Annis; Agnes (rare in south, 1650-1820); Anne
Alannus - Alan (Scots and northern)
Alicia (rare *Alitia*) - Alice (sep. name late C19)
Aloysius - (Ir); occasionally for Lewis, (W) Llewelyn
Ambilla - Mabel (rare)
Ambrosius - Ambrose; (W) Emrys
Amia - Amy
Amicia, Amissa - Amice, Ames (obs.)
Andreas - Andrew, Drew
Anna - Anne; Hannah; Nancy (sep. name late C18)
Antonius - Ant(h)ony
Arturus - Arthur
Audiarna,-ana - Odierne (obs.), rev. in diminutive Odette C20
Audria - Audrey
Avicia,-tia - Avis, Avice
Barnabus,-as - Barnaby, Barnabus
Bartolomaeus - Bartholomew, Bartelmey
Beatrix - Betteris (obs.) later revised as Beatrice in mid-C19 and sep. name C20
Benedictus - Bennet; Benedict
Beniaminus - Benjamin
Brigitta - Bridget
Caecilia - Cisley, Cicely (sep. late C19)
Caelia - Celia; (Ir) Sile, Sheila
Caritas - Charity
Carolus - Charles; (Ir) Turlough
Catalina - Catherine (rare)
Catalinis - Cataline (very rare)
Catherina - Katherine, Kate, Caitlin

Cata/ivellaunus - (W) Cadwallader (v rare)
Cecilia - Cecily, Cisley (sep. late C19)
Christi(a)na - Christian; sep. name (Sc) late C18; Eng. late C19
Christopherus - Christopher
Clemens - Clement (m)
Clementia - Clemency (rare f)
Coelia - Celia, Ceely; (Ir) Sile, Sheila
Constantia - Constance (sep. late C19)
Constans, Constantius - Constant (rare male name)
Cornelius - Cornelis, Cornelius; (Ir) Conn or Connor
Crispianus - Crispin (obs. 1600-1800)
Cristoverus - Christopher (bad form)
Cutbartus,-bertus, Cuthbertus, Cudbertus - Cuthbert
Danielis - Daniel; occas. (Sc) Donald; (Ir) Donough
Davidus - David
Diana - Diana, Dinah
Dionysia - Denis (f) rare after 1700
Dionysius - Denis (m) v rare except (Ir)
Dorothea - Dorothy (sep. name C18)
Drogo - Drew, Drury (rare)
Dulcia - Dowse (rare, obs. after 1600) rev. as Dulcie C19
Edmondus - Edmund, Ned
Ed^{rus} - abbrev. of *Edwardus*
Edwardus, Edvardus - Edward, Ned
Egidius, Egidia - Giles (m) and (Sc)(f)
Elena - Ellen, Helen; (Ir) Eileen
Elinora, Elionora, Eleanora - Eleanor
Eliza, Elizabetha - Elizabeth, Betty
Emma - Em, Emme; sep. from late C18
Emmota - Emmot; diminutive of Em. (rare, S.W. England)
Etheldreda - Audrey (rare; sep. name from late C19)
Eugenius - Eugene (rare); (W.Ir) Owen; (Sc) Ewan

Eva - Eve (rare); (Ir) Aoife
Ezekias - Hezekiah
Ezekielis - Ezekiel
Felicia - Phillis (sep. name late C19)
Felix - Felix (m, rare)
Fenella - (Ir) Finola
Fida - Faith
Fidelia - Troth (rare C17)(sep. name
    late C19)
Florens - Florent, Florence (m)
    (Ir or very rare)
Franciscus.-a - Francis (m), Frances (f)
Fridericus, Federicus - Frederick (v rare)
Galfridus, Gaufridus - Godfrey, Geoffrey,
    Jeffrey
Gartruda, Gatharuda - Gertrude
Gasparus - Jasper (rare)
Georgius, Gorgius - George
Giraldus. Girardus - Gerald, Gerard
Grania - (Ir) Grainne
Gratia - Grace
Griselda - Grizzel (rare)
Gualcherus, Gualterius - Walter
Guido - Guy
Guinevra - Winifred; (W) Gwyneth;
    Jenifer
Gulielmus, Guglielmus - William
Hadrianus - Adrian
Hannor(i)a - (Ir) Hannah, Honor, Nora
Helena - Ellen, Helen; (Ir) Eileen
Henricus, Hericus - Harry, Henry
Hierimia/s - Jeremiah, Jeremy
Hieronimus - Jerome, Jeronimo, Jeremy
Hodierna - Odierne (rare)(see
    Audiarna)
Homfridus - Humphrey
Honor(i)a - Honor; (Ir) Nora
Hugo - Hugh; (Sc) Aodh
Humfridus - Humphrey
I = J - so see *Iana, Ieremia,*
    Ioannes, Ioanna, under *Jana, etc.*
Isabella - Isabel, Elizabeth
Ishachus, Isaakus - Isaac
Ja^{bus} - rare abbrev. form of *Jacobus,*
    not *Jabez*
Jacobus - James; rarely = Jacob;
    (Ir) Seumas; (Sc) Hamish
Jacoba - James, f Scots name, later
    Jamesina
Jana - Jane; Joan; (Sc) Jean;
    (W) Sian; (Ir) Sine, Sheena
Janetta, Jonetta - (Sc) Janet, Jennet
Jeremia/s - Jeremy, Jeremiah
Jeronimus - Jerome
Joannes - John

Joan^{is} - abbrev. for John's, not
    Joan's
Jocosa - Joyce
Jocosus - Jocelyn (m), Josselin (m)(rare)
Joh^{es}, Joh^{is} - abbrev. for John, John's
Johanna, Joanna - Joan; (W) Sian; (Ir)
    Sine; (sep. name mid-C18)
Joannes, Ioannes, Johanis - John; (W)
    Ifan, Evan; (Ir) Sean
Josephus - Joseph; (rare sep. name
    late C18)
Josias - Josiah; (rare sep. name early C19)
Josua - Joshua
Judia - Judy, Judith
Juliana - Jill, Gillian
Julianus - Julian (m) (v rare)
Kat(h)arina, Katalina - Catharine;
    (Ir) Kait, Caitlin
Laura, Lavra - Lore (obs.); (sep.
    name C19)
Laurentius, Lavrentius - Laurence
Leon(h)ardus, Lionardus, Lennardus
    - Leonard
Lucas - Luke; sep. name possibly from
    surname C19
Lucia - Lucy; sep. name late C18
Lud/Lodovicus - Lewis, Louis; (W)
    Llewelyn; (sep. name Ludovic late C19)
Marcus - Mark; (sep. name late C19)
Maria - Mary; (sep. name late C19)
Marian(n)a - Marian, Mary Ann (sep.
    name late C19)
Marina = born at or by the sea
Martinus - Martin
Matilda, Matildis - Maud (obs. 1600-
    1850); (sep. name c1820)
Mattheus, Matthias - Matthew
Matthia, Martha - Martha
Mauritius, Mavritius - Maurice;
    (W) Morris
Misericordia - Mercy
Micaelis - Michael
Nicholas/-aus - Nicholas; Colin
Odiarna - Odiarne (obs.); revived
    diminutive Odette C20
Offylus - illiterate form of
    Theophilus
Oliverus - Oliver
Ollaferus - illiterate form of Oliver
Omfridus, Onfridus - Humphrey
Onoria - Honor; (Ir) Nora
Patientia - Patience
Patricius/-zius - Patrick
Peregrinus/a - Peregrine; lit. = a
    traveller, gipsy child

Petronella - Parnel (f) (obs.)

Petrus - Peter; Pierce

Philẹmo(n) - (Ir) Phelim

Phillida - Phillis; (sep. name from late C19)

Philippa - Philip (f) (obs.); (sep. name late C19)

Phillipus - Philip (m)

Placentia - Pleasance, Pleasant (f)

Radulphus - Ralph

Rainuldus - Reynell, Reynold

Randulphus/-olphus - Randolf, Randall (Cheshire)

Ranulphus - Reynold, Reynell, Rennell

Reginaldus - Reynell, Reynold; (sep. name late C19)

Ricardus - Richard

Robertus - Robert (also Rupert)

Spes - Hope (f) with *Caritas*, *Fida* for triplets

Stephanus - Stephen, Steven

Terentius - Terence

Thomas/Thoma - Thomas

Thomasina - Tomasin, Thomson (f); (sep. name late C19)

Timotheus - Timothy

Tobias - Toby; (sep. name C18)

Umfridus, Unfridus - Humphrey

Ursula - Ursley, Ursula

Wido - Guy (rare)

Willielmus - illiterate form of William

Wilmota, Guilmota - Willmott (south-west England)

Xpianus - Crispian, Crispin (obs. 1625-1895)

Xtopherus, Xoferus, Xpoferus - Christopher

Xtianus/a - Christian (m or f)

How these names are used in the registers

In a baptism, the child's name may appear as above (in the **nominative** form), but the father's and mother's names will be in the **genitive** (possessive) form. All names ending in '*-us*' in the nominative end in '*-i*' in the genitive:

> *Ricardus filius Ricardi Jones* = Richard son of Richard Jones.

> *Maria filia Timothei Smith* = Mary daughter of Timothy Smith.

All names ending in '*-es*' or '*-is*' become '*-is*' in the genitive form, so

> *Johannes filius Johannis Brown* = John son of John Brown.

All names ending in '*-a*' become '*-ae*' in the genitive, so

> *Maria filia Edwardi et Margaretae Green* = Mary the daughter of Edward and Margaret Green.

All names ending in '*-o*' add '*-nis*' in the genitive, so

> *Jacobus filius Hugonis Black* = James son of Hugh Black.

All names ending in '*-ix*' become '*-icis*' in the genitive, so

> *Fida filia Jacobi et Beatricis West* = Faith daughter of James and Betteris West.

The odd ones out are the men's names which end in '*-as*', like *Thomas*, *Tobias*, *Nicholas* or *Jeremias*. Sometimes they are treated as if they were female names and end in '*-ae*' in the genitive:

> *Micaelis filius Thomae North* = Michael son of Thomas North.

The commonest names occur so often that the clerks tended to abbreviate them, by writing the first syllable, then the ending, written small and higher than the name:

> *Joh^{es} filius Joh^{is}* = John son of John;

> *Ric^{us} filius Mic^{is}* = Richard son of Michael;

> *Rad^{us} filius Gul^{i}* = Ralph son of William.

Strictly, when a person is referred to as having something happen to him or her, as when John Smith married Mary Jones, her name should appear in the **accusative** case. Names ending in '*-a*' then become '*-am*', so Mary appears as:

> *Joh. Smith nupsit Mariam Jones* = John Smith married Mary Jones.

Names ending in '*-ix*', the other usual female ending, become '*-icem*':

> *Duxit in matrimonium Gulielmus Green Beatricem Brown* = William Green married Betteris Brown (lit., he led her into matrimony).

The same ought to happen when someone is baptised or buried, names ending in '*-us*' would then end in '*-um*'; names ending in '*-es*' and '*-is*' become '*-em*':

> *Sepultavi Johannem Smith filium Johnanni* = I buried John Smith son of John.

But for every clergyman who could handle such complications, there were twenty who chickened out and managed to avoid the confrontation with grammar by turning round the phrase to make it 'John Smith was buried' or by cutting off the endings. Naturally, he could claim he did this to save space. Sometimes there is such an effort at economy that all the unnecessary bits are omitted.

> *Rad. fil. Gul* = Ralph son of William.
> *Tho. fil. Joh*^{is} = Thomas son of John.

or even

> *Rad. fil. Gul.*

or

> *Tho. fill. Joh.*

You will notice that this caused the writers less problem, since they didn't have to remember how to decline the word correctly. And it is very convenient, for we don't have to either.

Once you have the names sorted out, that is half the battle. Then you will want to know what happened to them.

Baptisms

The page may be headed:

> *Nomina Baptizatorum* = The names of the baptised persons

(which avoids any need to go into the accusative case) or the entries may be labelled individually:

> *baptizat, baptizatur, baptizatus, baptizata est/erat; baptiz.*

Other expressions which may be found among the baptism entries include:

natus = born (a male)
nata = born (a female)
natus et renatus = born and reborn (i.e. baptised)
natus, renatus et denatus = born, baptised and 'de-born' or died
compatres = godparents

natu maior/major = the older born (of twins)
natu minor = the younger
natu maximus = the eldest born
domi = (baptised) at home
in extremis = on point of death
publice recepit = received into church

Marriages

Matrimonimum solemnizat = marriage was performed
X nupsit Y; X et Y nupserunt; nupti erant = X married Y (accusative); X and Y were married
nomina copulatorum = names of those joined in matrimony
ex (archi)episcopo = from the (arch)bishop
ex archidiacono = from the archdeacon
alias = otherwise known as

in matrimonium conjugati sunt; coniuncti erant; coniuxi; copulati sunt/erant = they were joined in matrimony
duxit in matrimonium = led into marriage
in vinculis matrimonii = in chains of marriage
per bannam/licentiam = by banns/licence
ex manibus archiepiscopi Cantuariensis/ Eboraciensis = from the hands of the (officials of the) Archbishop of Canterbury/York.

Burials

Sepultat; sepultabat; sepultatus est/ erat = he was buried
mortuus est/obiit = he/she died
occisit = he was killed
subito, repente, inopinato = suddenly
aetatis suae (XXX) annis = in the (thirtieth year of his age (see below, 'Time and Number' and page 10, 'The year of his age').
de mana sua (manis suis) = by his own hands
felo de se = suicide
in proelio = in battle
iuravit in forma legis/affidavit in forma legis = he/she swore in form of law/ an affidavit was made in legal form

corpus = the body
inhumabat = he was placed in the ground
exhumabatur et ad Londinium portatus est = he/she/it was dug up and carried to London (for reburial)
nihil nisi lana = in wool only
in tumulo antecessorum positum est = he was placed in the tomb (vault) of his forefathers
dormit = he is sleeping
iacebat in terram = he was thrown into the ground (a Dissenter)
interrebat/interruit sine ceremonio = he was interred without a service (for a Nonconformist or an excommunicated person).

There may be extra comments about the person's origins:

Place

In hac ecclesia = in this church
in hac parochia = in this parish
in hac urbe = in this town
in hoc vico = in this village, district
in hac vicinitate = in this neighbourhood
in hoc pago = in this village
in hoc loco = in this place
in comitatu = in the county of ...
coram publice = in public
domi = at home
hic = here

ibi = there
de = of
ex = from
ibid(em) = of/in the same place
praedictus = aforesaid
ambo = both
unus de ... alter de ... = one from ... the other from ...
Joh. Smith de Stangate in hac parochia et Maria Jones ibid. copulati sunt = John Smith of Stangate in this parish married Mary Jones of the same place.

After place names:

Parva = Little, small
Magna = Great, large
Superior = Upper
Inferior = Lower
in partibus australis = in the southern part(s) (of the parish, *etc.*), **not** in Australian parts
Anglia = England

orientalis = east(ern)
borealis = north(ern)
australis = south(ern)
occidentalis = west(ern)

Scotia = Scotland

Monachorum = (of the) Monks
Regis = King's
Abbatis = Abbot's
Episcopi = Bishop's
ex parte orientale = on/from the eastern side
super/juxta Mare = on/next the sea
Gwallia = Wales   *Hibernia* = Ireland

Entries from the baptism and marriage registers of All Saints, Oxford. '*Annoque praedicto*' means 'in the year aforesaid'. Note the use of the regnal year, '*ano regis Jacobi 5to*', in the lower example.

Time and Number

ante = before
post = after
hora = hour   dies = day
  usually met with as in:
eodem die = on the same day (as the
  last event)
proximo die/mensis/anno = on the next
  day/month/year
ultimo die mensis (Octobris) = on the
  last day of (October)
Anno Domini = in the year of our Lord
prima luce = at first light

ante meridiem = before noon (a.m.)
post meridiem = afternoon (p.m.)
mensis = month   annus = year

eodem mense/anno = in the same
  month/year
eadem hora = in the same hour
primo die mensis (Aprilis) = on the
  first day of the month of (April)
anno praedicto (or predicto) = in the
  aforesaid year
noctu, nocte = by or at night.

Dates are often expressed in Latin numbers:

NUMBER	otherwise written as	NUMBER	otherwise written as
i	primo (on the 1st)	xi	undecimo (on the 11th)
ii/ij	secundo (on the 2nd)	xii	duodecimo (on the 12th)
iii/iij	tertio (on the 3rd)	xiii	decimo tertio (on the 13th)
iv/iiij	quarto (on the 4th)	xiv	decimo quarto (on the 14th)
v	quinto (on the 5th)	xv	decimo quinto (on the 15th)
vi	sexto (on the 6th)	xvi	decimo sexto (on the 16th)
vii	septimo (on the 7th)	xvii	decimo septimo (on the 17th)
viii	octavo (on the 8th)	xviii	decimo octavo (on the 18th)
ix	nono (on the 9th)	xix	decimo nono; or undevicesimo (on the 19th)
x	decimo (on the 10th)		
xx	vicesimo (vigesimo, rare)(on the 20th)	xxx	tricesimo (trigesimo, rare) (on the 30th)
xxi	vicesimo primo (on the 21st) and so on until	xxxi	trecesimo primo (on the 31st)
xxix	vicesimo nono or undetricesimo (on the 29th)		

Actual numbers are:

1 *unus*	2 *duo*	3 *tres*	4 *quattuor*	5 *quinque*
6 *sex*	7 *septem*	8 *octo*	9 *novem*	10 *decem*

When the English church year began in March (until 1752), September was the seventh month, and so on to December, the tenth month. This is why you will sometimes find the months written as '7ber', '8ber', '9ber', '10ber', which should be read as September, October, *etc.*, not the present 7th month, July, *etc.*

C = centum, 100   CC = 200 and so on   L = 50
XC = 10 before 100, so 90   XL = 10 before 50, so 40
M = mille, 1000   D = dimidium, half (of M), so 500
l = libra, a pound (weight, lb.) or £ (money)
s = solidus, a shilling   d = denarius, a penny
summa tota or in toto = the whole sum, in total.

Sometimes, mostly in or before the sixteenth century, dates are given as Saints' days. The full list can be checked in *Whitaker's Almanack*, but the commoner ones in English church usage are:

die natalis Domini (Dni) Christi Redemptoris mundi = on the birth day of our lord Christ, saviour of the world (December 25)

die feste Sanctae Virginis Mariae = on the feast day of the Blessed Virgin Mary (March 25)

die feste SS Philippi et Jacobi = the feast day of St Philip & St James (May 1, often the first day of the Easter Quarter Sessions)

feste Sancti Johannis = feast of St John (Baptist) (June 24)

feste Sancti Micaelis = feast of St Michael (September 25)

Regnal Years

In some documents, including many older printed pedigrees, events may be dated according to the **regnal years** of various monarchs with their name written in abbreviated Latin e.g.

10 Eliz; 5 Hen VIII; 2 Jac II; 10 Geo IV; 24 Vic.

The thing to watch for is that the first day of the reign starts year one, so *10 Geo IV* (1820 - 1830) is 1820 +9 = 1829, not 1830. The reign started on the day of proclamation (before Edward I, on the coronation day) so if an exact day is stated, beware.

26 October *5 Geo III* = 1760 +4 = 1764

24 October *5 Geo III* is not two days earlier, but 364 days later, since George II died in the morning of October 25.

For a ull list of regnal years with official commencement dates, see john Richardson's *Local Historian's Enclylopedia* (sect. D.) or that made by Robert Massey in *Origins* (Bucks FHS Vol 2 no 1). Accession dates can also be obtained from royal genealogies in *Burke's Peerage*.

The Year of His Age

Where ages are given in burials (usually of the gentry), these may be expressed as

aetatis suae xl (annos/is) = in the fortieth year of his age.

This may be abbreviated to *aet. xl.* We enter our first year as soon as we are born, so this is 39, rising 40, not 40 at the moment.

Roman Calendar

A very few really learned Classics men occasionally used the old Roman names for days. The basic days were:

Kalends = 1st day   *Nones* = 5th day   *Ides* = 13th day of month

'Calendar' is taken from *Kalends*. All other days were reckoned as:

a(nte) d(iem) iii nonas = 3 days before Nones = the 3rd (counting the days at either end.

In the 'long' months, the dates changed. Remember it as
'In March, July, October, May,   *Nones* on the 7th, *Ides* on the 15th day'.

You are very unlikely to meet this sort of dating, except in the university cities. A detailed explanation is given by Cedric Watts in the *Oxfordshire Historian* vol 2 no 4 (Spring 1981).

You may sometimes see a reference to 'the Greek *Kalends*'. There isn't one. A promise to pay on that day meant 'never'.

Illegitimacy and Strangers

Johannes filius Mariae Jones et reputat(ur) de Johanni Smith
= John son of Mary Jones and by repute of John Smith (i.e is certain)
Johannes fil. Mariae Green et imputat de Ricardo Brown
= John son of Mary Green and, she claims, of Richard Brown (i.e.probably)
filius nullius = son of none (the girl didn't say)
filius populi = son of the people (anybody's guess of six)
filius cuiusdam peregrini/ae = son of a certain travelling man/woman
nomine ignoto = (with) his name unknown *gnothus,ignotus* = unknown,base
(nomine) Ricardus vel Diccon = named Richard or Dicky
ut fertur = as it is said (i.e.believe it if you like)
dictus, p(rae)dictus = the said, aforesaid (man) *vocatus* = called, known as

Status & Professions, the nobility, gentry, and wealthy

Rex, Regina = King, Queen

Dux, ducis = Duke, of the Duke (lit = leader)

Comes, comitis = Earl, of the Earl

Vi(ce)comes = Viscount

Baronettus = Baronet

Dominus (Dns) = Lord, Sir; pre 1600, hon. title for clergyman

Domina (Dna.) = Lady (wife of Lord); Dame (wife of knight)

Dominus huius locus = lord of (the manor in)this place

eques = knight; cavalry officer (lit. horseman)

miles,militis = lit. soldier, of a soldier; knight, Sir

armiger = person entitled to bear arms

gentis,ex gente = of the race of

generosus/a = gentleman/lady (by birth, later by wealth)

cl(er)icus = cleric, clergyman not parish clerk

Doctor = of divinity, laws, not normally of medicine

Magister Artium = master of Arts, with university degree

magister, M = Master, extended as mere title of respect to gentry or local rich man

Cives et (trade) = Citizen and (trade) of London, Freeman of the livery company indicated

patronus huius ecclesiae patron (appointer of parson) of this church

stirps; ex stirpe = . offspring, lineage; of the (direct) family of

Relationships and Age Descriptions

amita - paternal aunt
ancilla - servant maid
anus - old woman (very rare)
antecessores - ancestors
ava - grandmother
avunculus - maternal uncle
avus - grandfather
coelebs - bachelor
cohaeres - joint heiress
coniunx - spouse (f)
consanguineus/a - m/f cousin, blood
    relative; any relation except parent,
    brother or sister, including grand-
    children, niece or nephew
consobrinus - see *sobrinus*
cuiusdam - genitive of *quidam*
domesticus - inmate of the house
eius - his, that person's
familia - extended family + servants,
    household
famulus - servant in the house
filia - daughter
filia sororis - sister's daughter, niece
filia unica - sole daughter
filiola - small daughter of
filiolus - small son of
filius - son
filius et haeres - son and heir
filius fratris - brother's son, nephew
filius naturalis - natural born son; in
    wills, son by blood, not stepson nor
    son in law
filius nullius/populi - see page 11
frater - brother
gemini, gemelli - twins (see *natu maior*)
gener - son in law
gens, gentis - (of) the race (of)
germanus/a - m/f close blood kin, own
    sibling
gnothus - illegitimate
haeres, heredes - heir, heiress/heirs
homo, homines - man, men in general,
    people (*cf. vir*)
ignotus - unknown
ille - that person
illegitimus - bastard
imputat(ur) - it is claimed
iunior, junior - younger
iuvenis - youth, about 13 to 20
liberi, liberorum - (plural) children,
    of the children (compare *liber, libri,
    librorum* - a book, books, of books)
mater - mother

mater mea - my mother
matertera - maternal aunt
maximus - the oldest of three
    (*e.g.* grandfather)
meus, mea - adj. my
natu maior, major - older born of twins
natu maximus, minimus - oldest, youngest
    born
natu minor - younger born of twins
nepos, nepotes - grandchild, grand-
    children (very rarely, a nephew)
neptis - (rarely) a niece
nurus - daughter in law
Orbus, orba - m/f orphan
parvu(lu)s - (very) small, weak, young
pater - father
pater familias - householder
pater suus - his own father
patruelis - cousin on the father's side
patruus - paternal uncle
praedictus/a - m/f the person mentioned
    above
privigna - step daughter
privignus - step son
proavus - great grandfather
proles - issue, descendants
puella - girl, about 5 to 12
puellula - tiny girl
puer - boy, about 5 to 12
puerulus - tiny boy
quidam - a certain; *cuiusdam* - of a
    certain (man, traveller, *etc.*)
relicta - left-behind; widow
reputat(ur) - it is legally presumed
senex - an old man
senior - older
servus - male servant
sobrinus, consobrinus - cousin on the
    mother's side
socer - father in law
socrus/ra - mother in law
solutus/a - m/f unmarried
soror - sister
spurius - bastard
suus, sua - his, her very own
unigena/itus/a - born at a birth
uxor - wife
uxor eius - wife of the man mentioned
    above, his wife
vidua - widow
vir - individual man, husband
virgina - maiden, about 13 to 20
virgina antiqua - elderly spinster

Trades and Occupations

In most parishes, only a handful of these names will be used — but it will not necessarily be the same handful, so I have selected the ones most commonly used in different areas.

aedificator - builder, architect
aegyptianus - egyptian, gypsy
agricola - farmer, husbandman
architectus - mason, builder, bricklayer, and (rarely) architect
artifex - artisan
aurifex - goldsmith
bibliopola - bookseller
bladarius - corn chandler
brasiarius - maltster
burriarius - dairyman
calciarius - shoemaker
carbonarius - charcoal burner/seller, collier
clavifaber - nailmaker
clericus - clerk, normally clergyman, clerk in holy orders
clericus huius parochiae - clerk of (this) parish
cocus, coquus - cook
comedianus - actor
constabularius - constable
doctor - of divinity or laws, not medicine
emptor - buyer (with specified commodity)
faber - smith, used in combination for various artisans
faber aerarius - coppersmith, brazier
faber argentarius/aurantarius - goldsmith, silversmith
faber clavi, clavorum - nailmaker
faber clavarum - key-, locksmith
faber ferrarius - iron smith, blacksmith
faber lignarius - wood smith, carpenter
faber rotarius - wheelwright
fabrifer/ferrifaber - blacksmith, ironworker
figulus - potter
funerius - rope maker
fur - thief
furnarius - baker, furnace owner
g(u)ardianus - churchwarden, guardian
gregarius - drover, cattleman
horologiarius - clockmaker
hortulanius, hortarius - gardener
hostellarius - innkeeper
husbandus - husbandman, small farmer
itinerans/erarius - a traveller
laborarius - labourer
lanarius - weaver, strictly of wool; wool merchant

lanius, laniator - butcher
lapidarius - stonemason
ludimagister - schoolmaster (lit. master of games)
medicus/inus - physician
mercator - merchant
mercator pecoris - cattle jobber
meretrix - prostitute
miles/miletes - soldier/s (knight)
molendarius, molinarius - miller
molitor, molarius - millwright
nauta - sailor (m)
navigator - boatman, lighterman
notarius - lawyer, notary
nutrix - nurse, wetnurse
obstetrix - midwife
operarius, opifex - skilled workman, craftsman
ovium pastor - shepherd of sheep
paedogogus - schoolmaster
pannarius - cloth seller
pastor - shepherd
pauper - poor person
pecuarius - grazier
pellicarius - skinner
peregrinus/a - traveller (m/f)
pictor - painter
piscator - fisherman
pistor - baker
plebianus - common man; anyone with no coat of arms, even if rich
pomarius - fruit seller
porcorum emptor - pig buyer
restio - rope maker
rotarius - wheelwright
rusticus - countryman
saponarius - soap boiler
sartor - tailor
scissor - barber
scribus - scribe, scrivener
scriptor - the writer
stabularius - stable keeper, ostler
structor - builder, mason, bricklayer
sutor - shoemaker
tabernarius - taverner, innkeeper
tannarius - tanner
tector - plasterer
textor - weaver
tibialis factor - framework knitter, stockiner

tinctor - dyer	*vendor* - seller (+ commodity)
tonellarius - cooper, barrelmaker	*vestiarius* - clothier
tonsor - barber	*vitellarius* - victualler
vaccarius - cowman	*vitrarius* - glazier, glass seller

Probate of the will of Giles Franckling of New Woodstock, Oxon, 1665.
(Oxfordshire Record Office, MSS. Wills Oxon. 127/2/11, reproduced by kind permission)

Reading a Latin will probate

Precise phrasing varies from place to place, and words are often greatly abbreviated. It looks a fearsome sight, but you only need three, or even two, things — the name of the deceased, the date when it was proved, and the name/s of the executor/s. The rest is normally a piece of legal gobbledygook.

The name of the deceased may appear on line 1 or 2, *e.g.*

Rici Jarvis nuper de Haddenham Archinat. Buck. = Richard Jarvis
late of Haddenham in the Archdeaconry of Bucks.

In the example shown opposite (top), we omit the name and go straight into:

Probat(um) erat hoc T(estame)ntum apud Oxon. = Proved was this
Testament (will) at Oxford.

Then comes the date, *'decimo septo die mens(i)s Septembr(is) 1665'*, the 17th day of September 1665. The year may be written in Latin first but it is normally repeated in figures here or on the back of the will.

The next section is to the greater glorification of the official proving the will and can be ignored — unless, of course, you are related to the 'venerable man, Henry Alworth, doctor of laws and surrogate for Sir Giles Sweit, LL.D., officer of the Archdeaconry of Oxford'.

Look next for the name of the executor, more usually two to three lines from the bottom. Here the description is very much cut down as:

Petri Franckling fil(io) &c et un(o) Execut(orum) &c = Peter
Franckling son *etc* and one Executor.

The '*&c*' would normally be expanded to:

filio naturale et legitimo = (to the) natural and lawful son;
and
uno Executorum in hoc testamento nominato = (to) one of the
Executors nominated in this will.

Then come the standard probate clauses:

Cui com(m)issa fuit et est Ad(ministra)c(i)o(nem) Adco.
om(niu)m et singulor(um) bonor(um) &c = to whom was
committed Administration of all and every of the goods;
d(ic)to def(unc)ti et ei(u)s T(estame)ntum = of the said
deceased and his will;
qualiscumque concernen(tum) = (of) whatsoever it may concern;
in forma Juris Jurato Salve jure cuiuscu(m)que = in form of
law sworn by oath with whomsoever (concerning to deal) justly.

If '*affirmato*' or '*affirmavit*' appears instead of '*jurato*', then you have a Quaker as executor.

Unusually, it was witnessed:

in p(rese)ntia mei Nic: Horsman, Reg(ist)rarii.

This is where the ordinary probate entry finishes. The names of the executors should match exactly what is in the (English) body of the will.

Other forms of words often met are:

unico executore/unica executrice = by the sole (male) executor/ (female) executrix;

relicta defuncti [rlca dfti] = (by) the relict, widow of the deceased

If the names do not completely match those in the text, look for

executore substito = the surviving executor;

or *reservata, potestate reservata* as in

et reservata Elizabetha Frankling Ex(ecu)trici in hoc T(estame)nto etiam no(m)i(n)at = and power reserved to Elizabeth Frankling in this will also (as) Executrix nominated.

Notice the curvy line over *nominat* which shows that 'n' or 'm', or in this case, both, have been omitted.

This may be followed by a further grant, often much abbreviated, but in this case written out in full (lower section p.14), to the other executor. The second probate entry is dated 17 February 1665 - which is five months later, modern 1666 - and before Nicholas Vilett, LL.B. The will is proved in much the same words by Elizabeth:

ux(or)is et alterius execut' in hoc T(estame)nto no(m)i(n)at = the wife and the other (of two) executors named in the will.

She is sworn *bene et fidel(ite)r* = well and faithfully - to administer and (see to) *de solvendi Debita &c et legata &c* = paying of debts etc and legacies etc

Her oath is taken in the presence of Jo(hn) Rhodes *No. pubco* , Notary Public.

If the named executor/s die before taking administration, their own executors may do so. If the executor dies intestate, then the next of kin is granted administration. If the next of kin is under 21, then the next adult acts:

AB patruus eius (guardianus) causa minoritate Johannis B filius dicti defuncti = AB uncle on the father's side (guardian) by reason of the minority of John C son of the said deceased.

Sometimes not all of the legacies in the will are due until some years later, after the executor named has died. Administration will then be granted to his executor or next of kin as above

de bonis non = or goods not (distributed).

Administration follows a similar pattern if the executor is abroad or insane.

non compos mentis = not of whole mind.

If you see strange names and *creditores*, then the deceased died in debt and probate was granted to the principal creditor/s. If you find any other reasonably short form of words added to the probate entry, then it is best to ask the archivist for help. It may be a rewording of one of the phrases above.